SandCastle™
Capital Letters

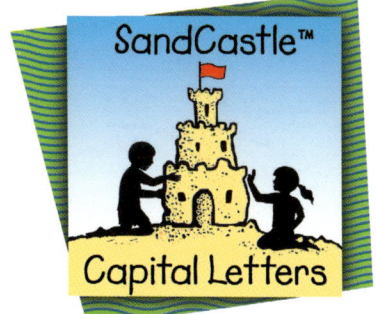

States

Pam Scheunemann

ABDO
Publishing Company

Published by SandCastle™, an imprint of ABDO Publishing Company, 4940 Viking Drive, Edina, Minnesota 55435.

Copyright © 2001 by Abdo Consulting Group, Inc. International copyrights reserved in all countries. No part of this book may be reproduced in any form without written permission from the publisher. SandCastle™ is a trademark and logo of ABDO Publishing Company.

Printed in the United States.

Cover and interior photo credits: Corel, Corbis Images, PhotoDisc

Library of Congress Cataloging-in-Publication Data

Scheunemann, Pam, 1955-
    States / Pam Scheunemann.
        p. cm. -- (Capital letters)
    Includes index.
    ISBN 1-57765-613-X (hardcover)
    ISBN 1-59197-101-2 (paperback)
        1. English language--Capitalization--Juvenile literature. 2. U.S. states--Juvenile literature. 3. Names, Geographical--Juvenile literature. [1. English language--Capitalization. 2. United States. 3. Names, Geographical.] I. Title. II. Series.

PE1450 .S347 2001
428.1--dc21

2001022895

The SandCastle concept, content, and reading method have been reviewed and approved by a national advisory board including literacy specialists, librarians, elementary school teachers, early childhood education professionals, and parents.

Let Us Know

After reading the book, SandCastle would like you to tell us your stories about reading. What is your favorite page? Was there something hard that you needed help with? Share the ups and downs of learning to read. We want to hear from you! To get posted on the ABDO Publishing Company Web site, send us email at:

sandcastle@abdopub.com

About SandCastle™

A professional team of educators, reading specialists, and content developers created the SandCastle™ series to support young readers as they develop reading skills and strategies and increase their general knowledge. The SandCastle™ series has four levels that correspond to early literacy development in young children. The levels are provided to help teachers and parents select the appropriate books for young readers.

Emerging Readers
(no flags)

Beginning Readers
(1 flag)

Transitional Readers
(2 flags)

Fluent Readers
(3 flags)

These levels are meant only as a guide. All levels are subject to change.

ABDO Publishing Company

To see a complete list of SandCastle™ books and other nonfiction titles from ABDO Publishing Company, visit **www.abdopub.com** or contact us at:
4940 Viking Drive, Edina, Minnesota 55435 • 1-800-800-1312 • fax: 1-952-831-1632

Aa Bb Cc

States start with capital letters.

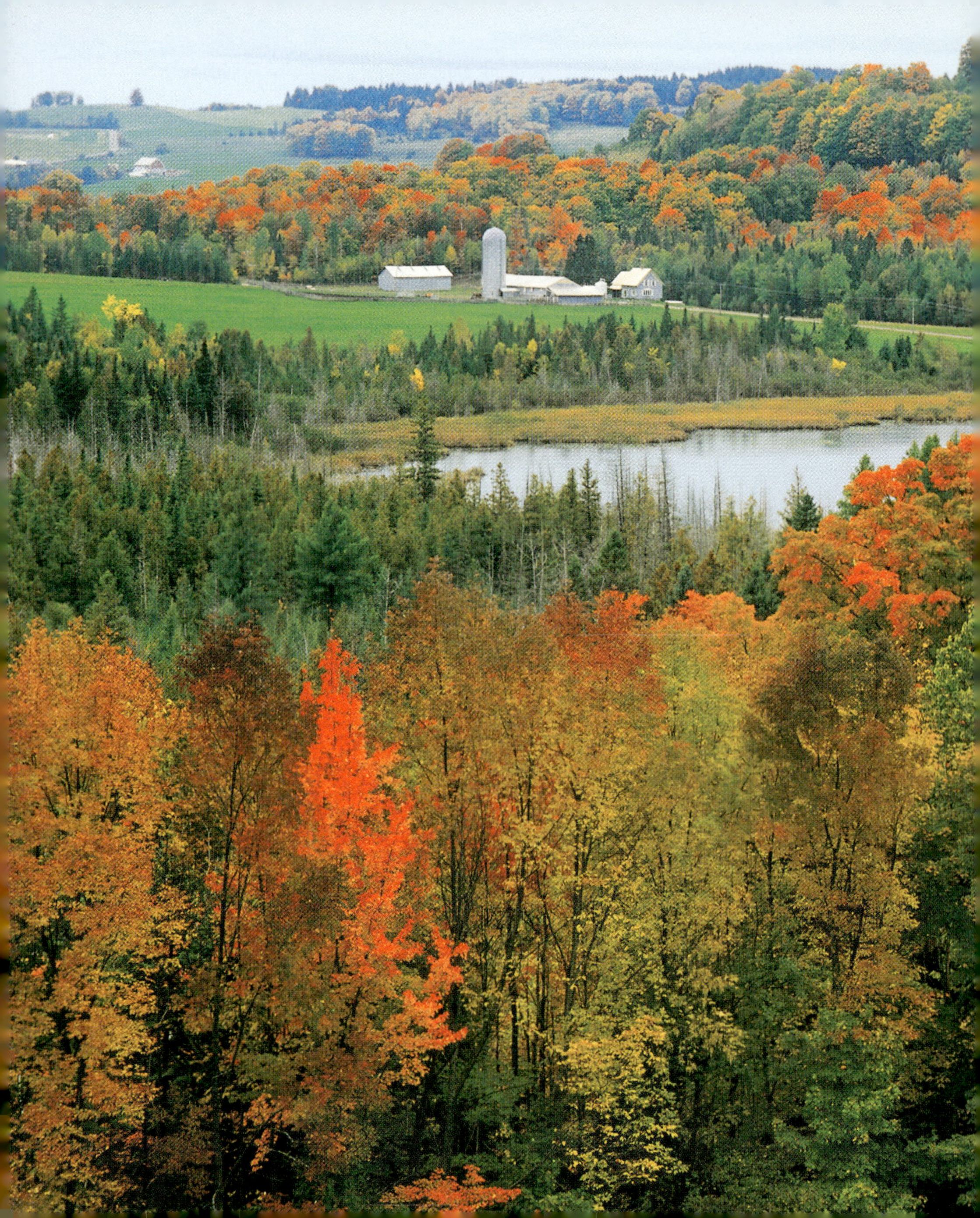

Aa Bb Cc

Fall is pretty in Vermont.

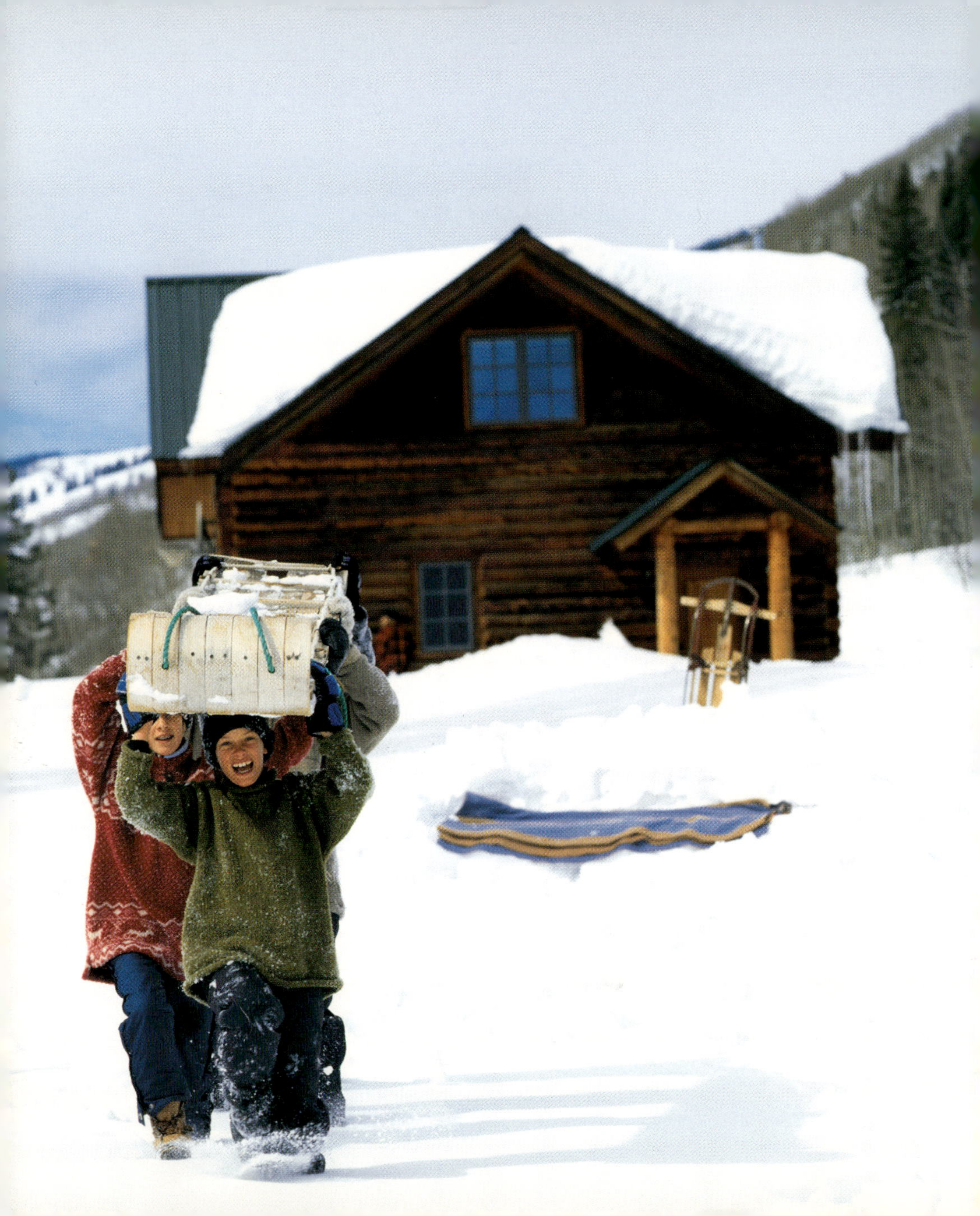

Aa Bb Cc

It snows in Colorado.

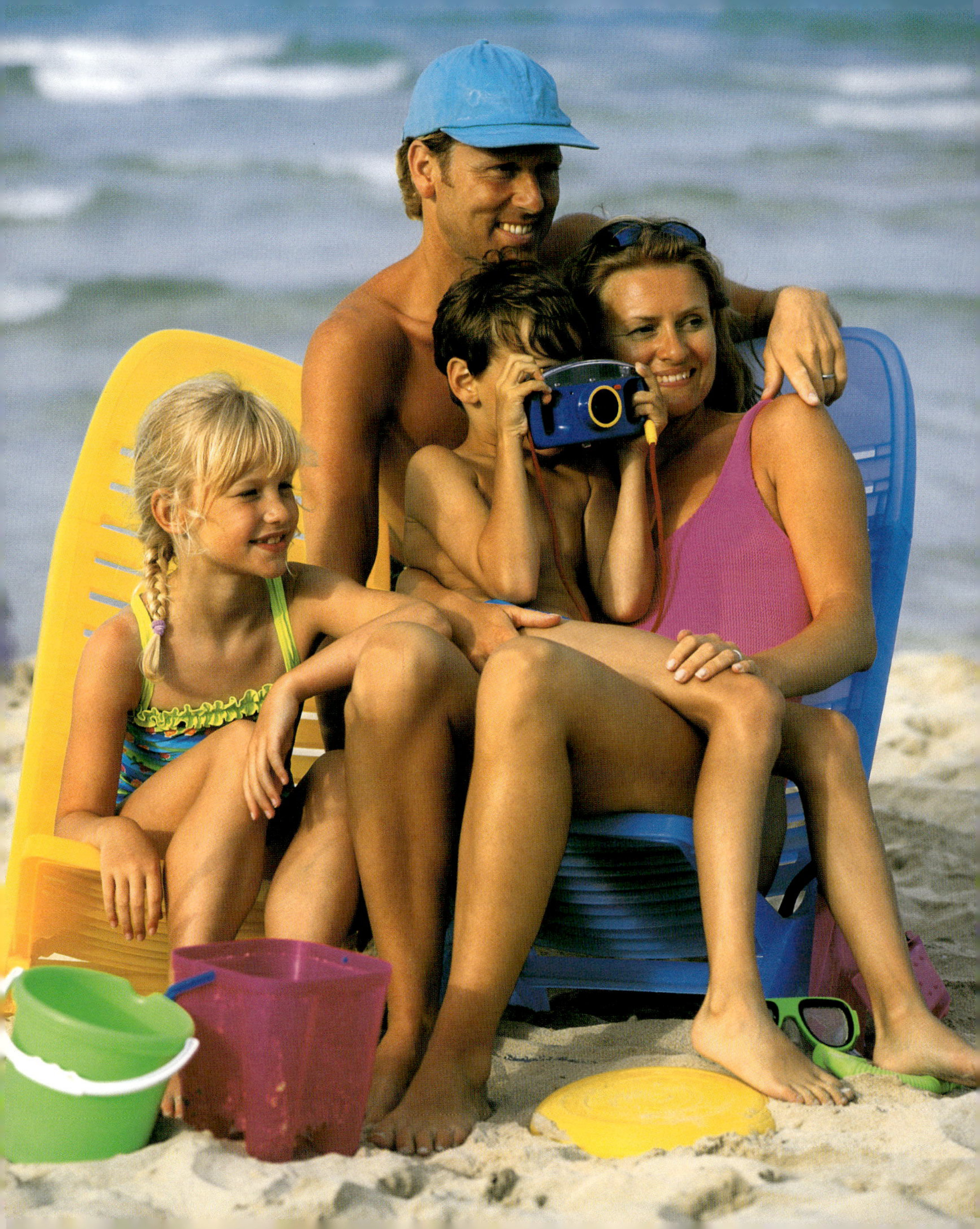

Aa Bb Cc

It is warm in Florida.

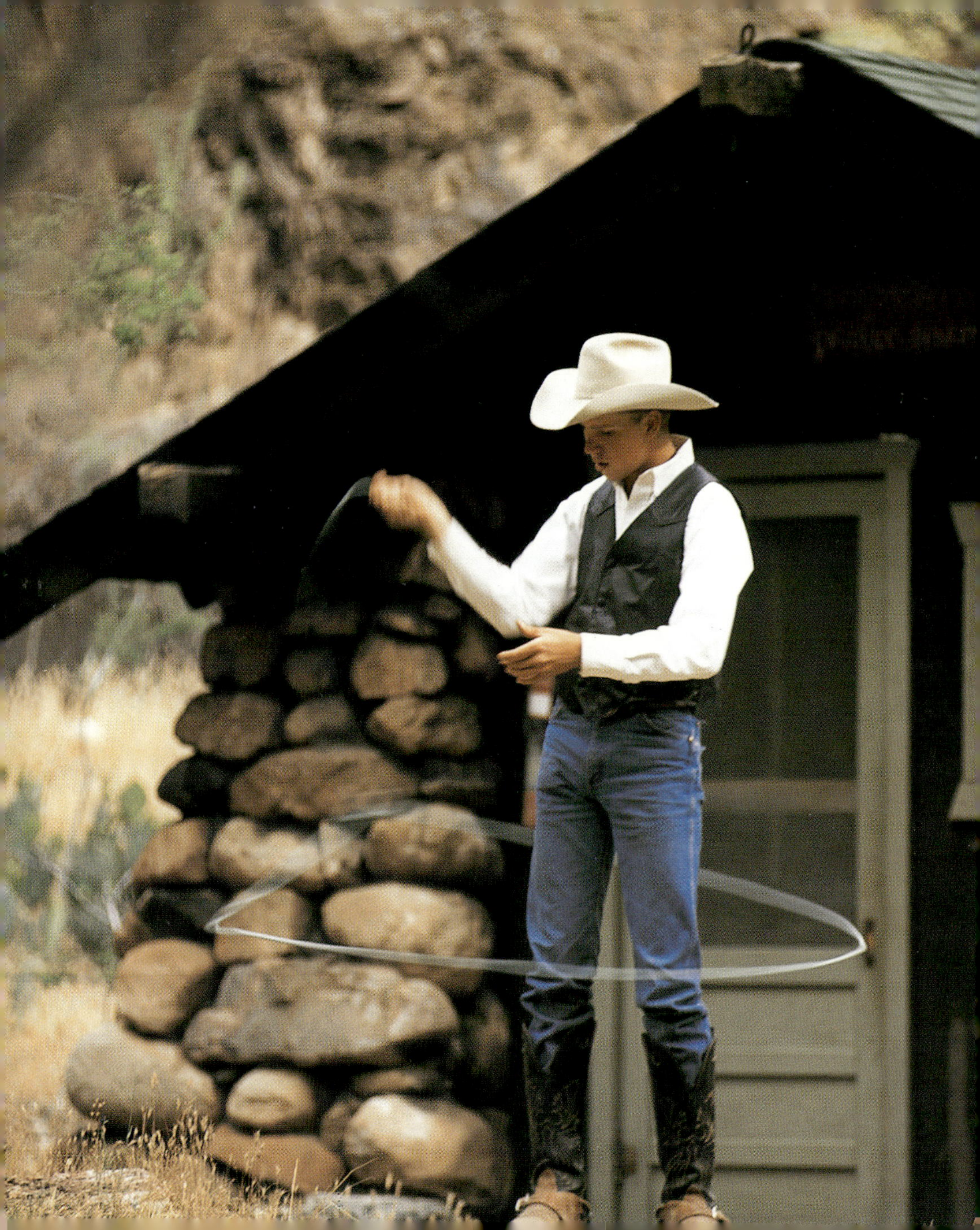

Aa Bb Cc

Some cowboys live in Texas.

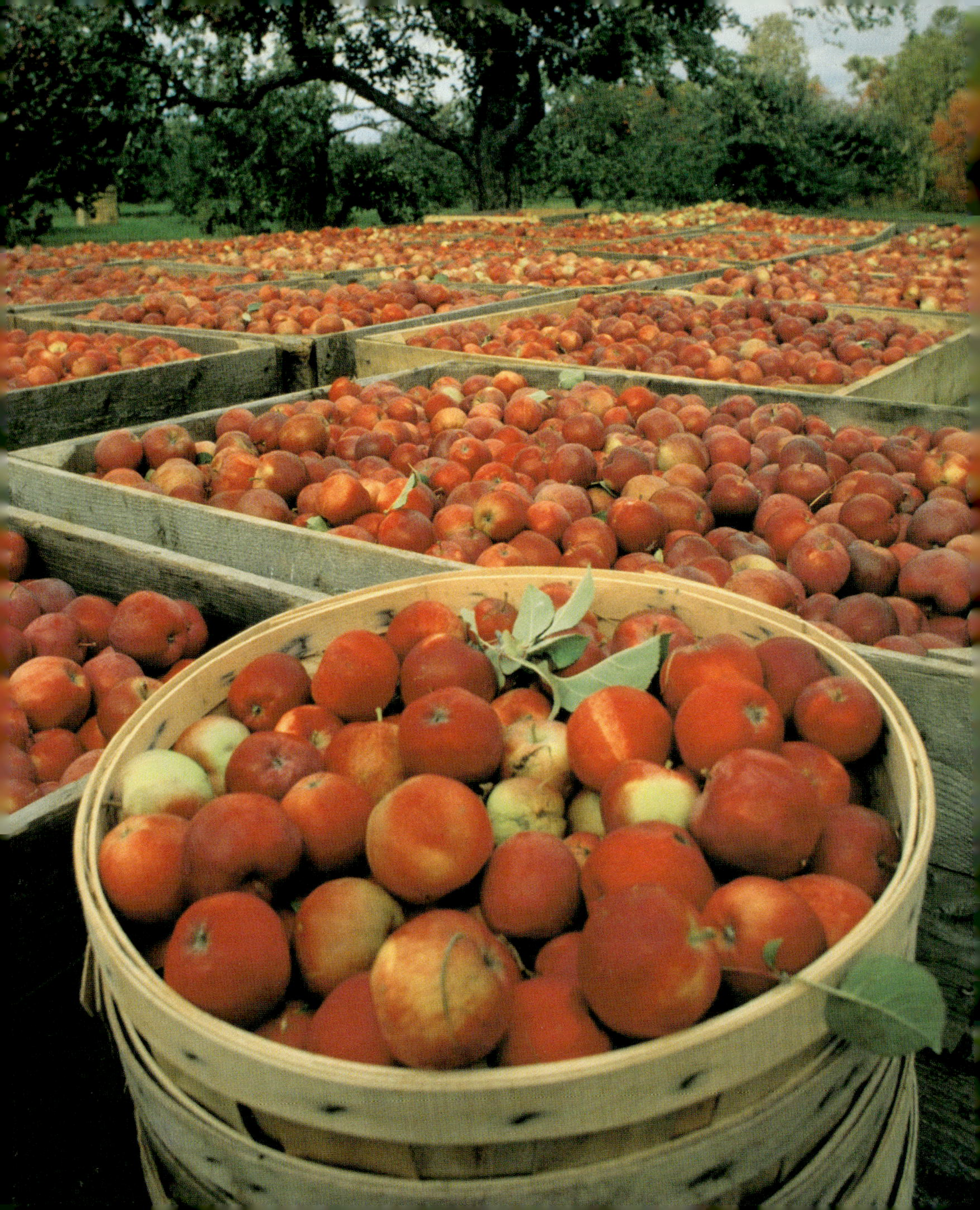

Aa Bb Cc

Apples grow in Washington.

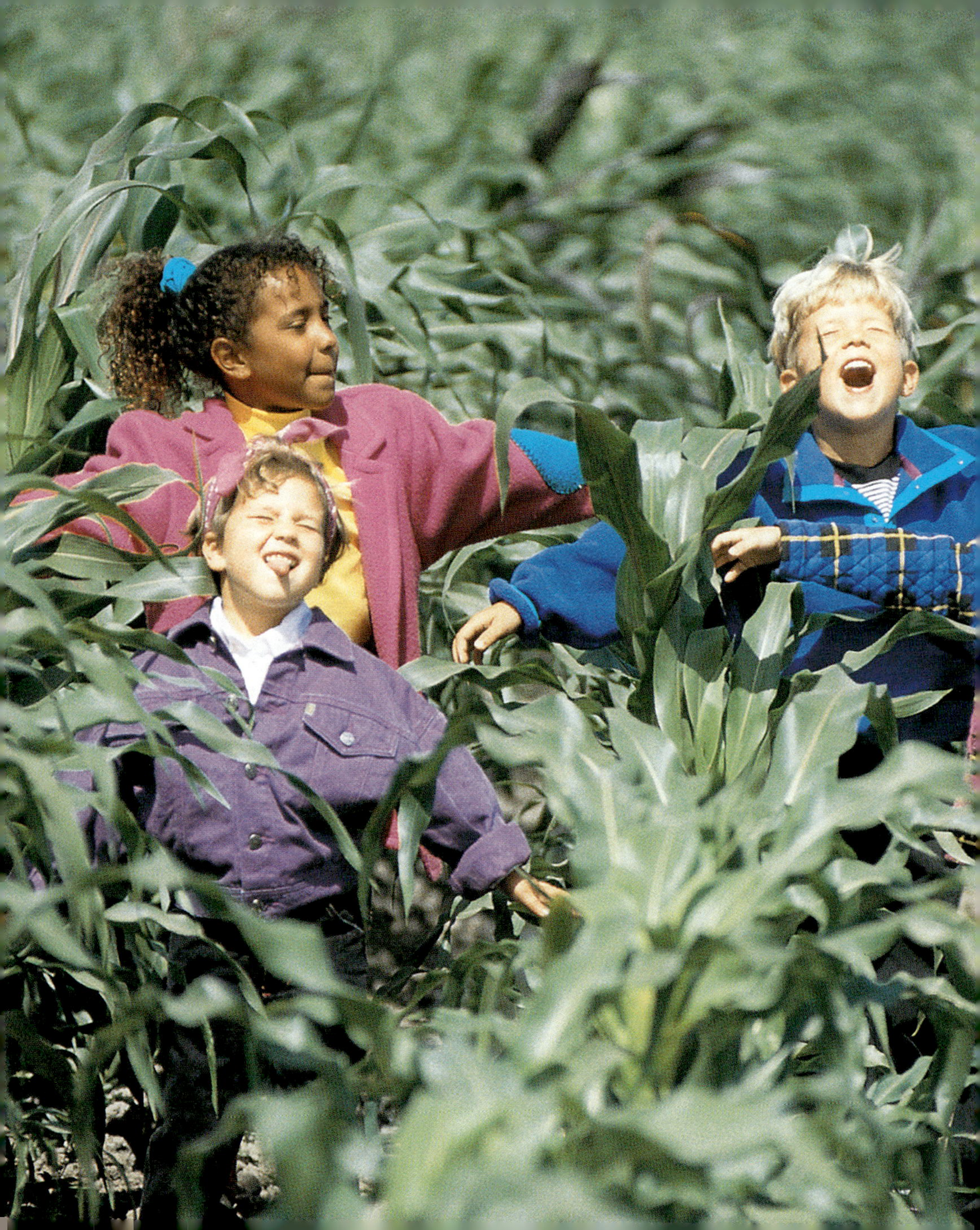

Aa Bb Cc

Corn grows in Iowa.

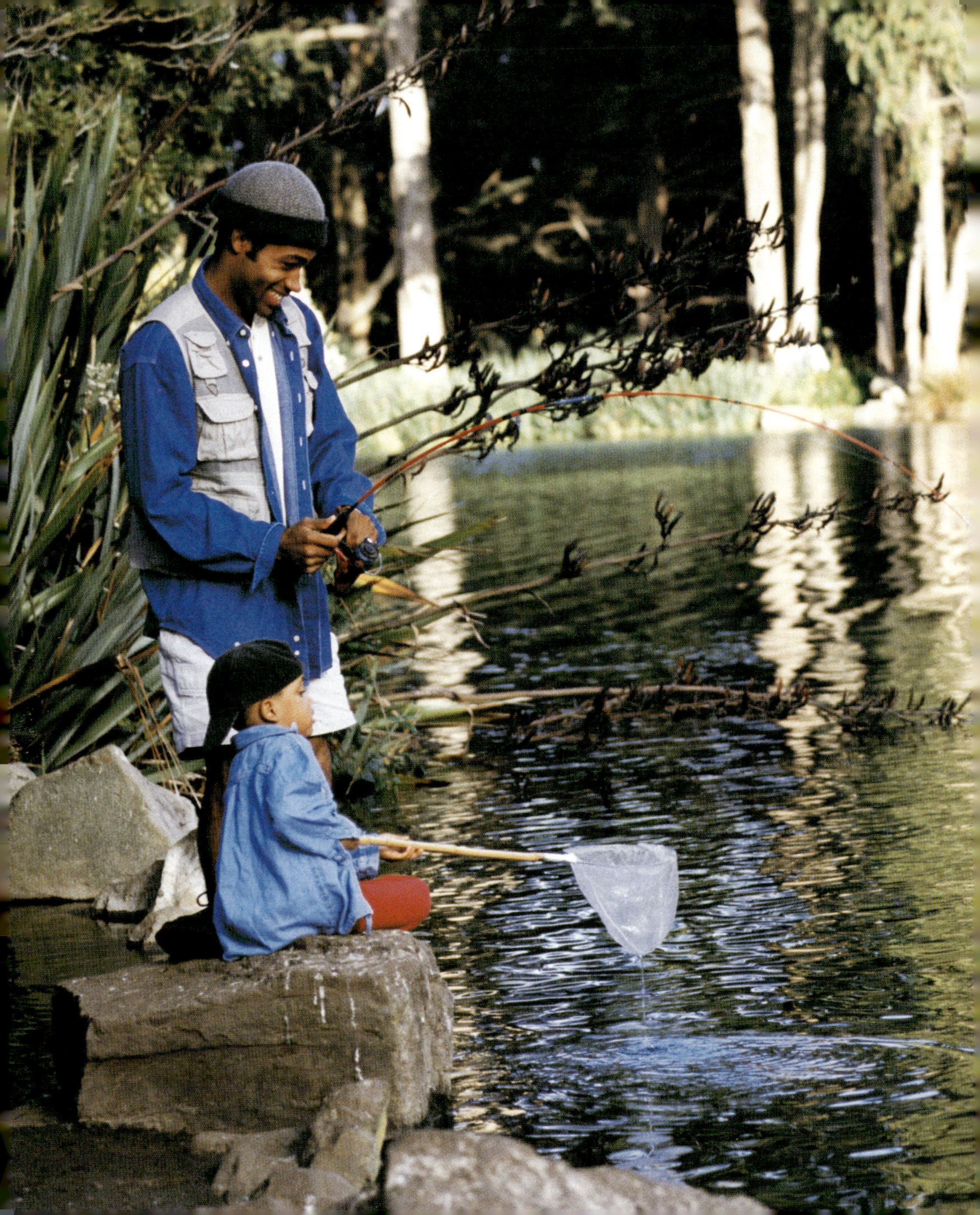

There are lakes in Minnesota.

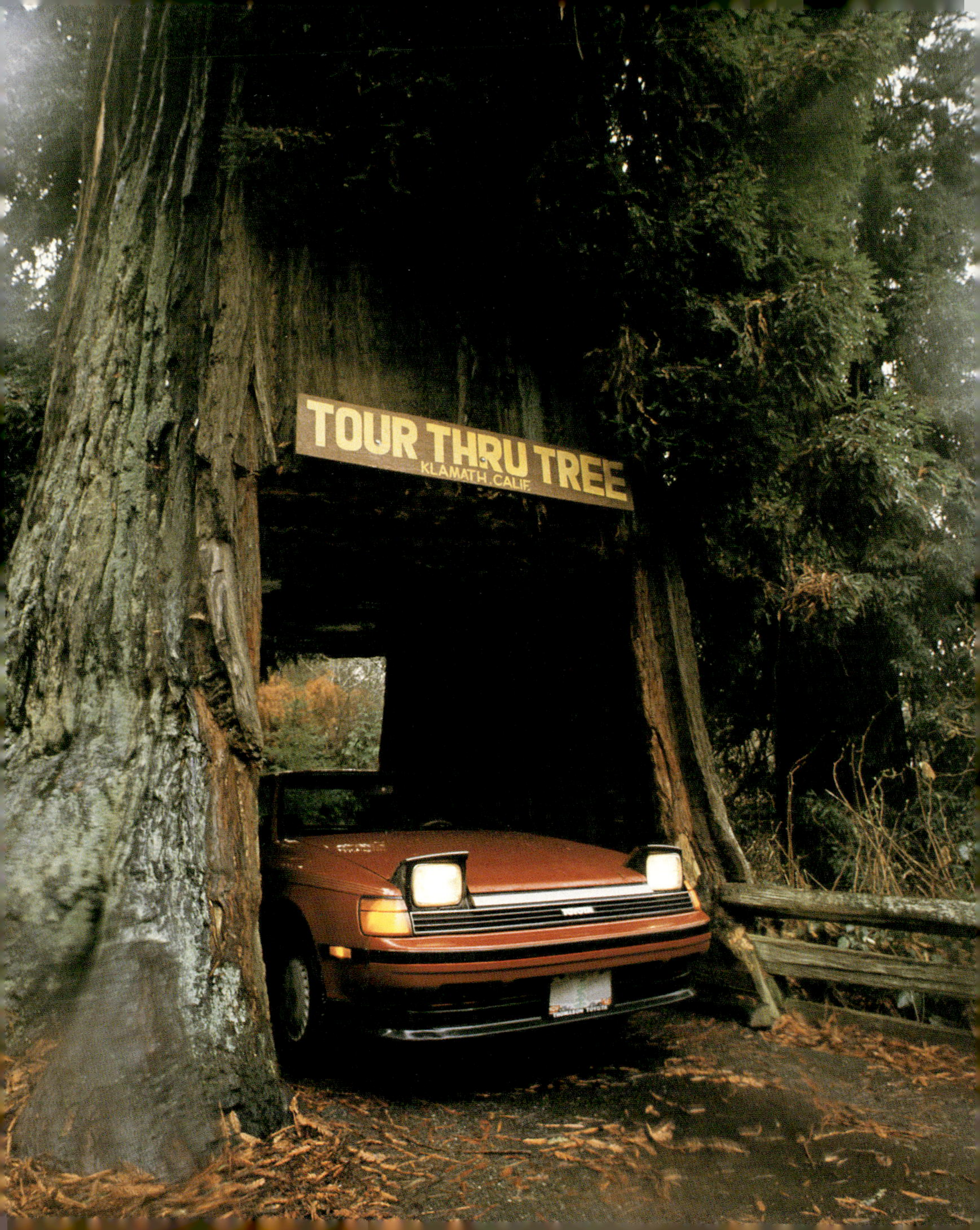
TOUR THRU TREE
KLAMATH, CALIF.

Aa Bb Cc

What letter does California start with?

(Capital C)

Words I Can Read

Nouns

A *noun* is a person, place, or thing
apples (AP-uhlz) p. 15
corn (KORN) p. 17
cowboys (KOU-boiz) p. 13
fall (FAWL) p. 7
lakes (LAKESS) p. 19
letter (LET-ur) p. 21
letters (LET-urz) p. 5
states (STATESS) p. 5

Proper Nouns

A *proper noun* is the name of a person, place, or thing
California (kal-i-FOR-nyuh) p. 21
Colorado (kol-ur-AD-oh) p. 9
Florida (FLOR-i-duh) p. 11
Iowa (EYE-uh-wuh) p. 17

Minnesota (min-uh-SOH-tuh) p. 19
Texas (TEKS-uhss) p. 13
Vermont (vuhr-MONT) p. 7
Washington (WOSH-ing-tuhn) p. 15

Verbs

A verb is an action or being word
are (AR) p. 19
does (DUHZ) p. 21
grow (GROH) p. 15
grows (GROHZ) p. 17
is (IZ) pp. 7, 11
live (LIV) p. 13
snows (SNOHZ) p. 9
start (START) pp. 5, 21

The United States

Alabama
Alaska
Arizona
Arkansas
California
Colorado
Connecticut
Delaware
Florida
Georgia
Hawaii
Idaho
Illinois
Indiana
Iowa
Kansas
Kentucky
Louisiana
Maine
Maryland
Massachusetts
Michigan
Minnesota
Mississippi
Missouri

Montana
Nebraska
Nevada
New Hampshire
New Jersey
New Mexico
New York
North Carolina
North Dakota
Ohio
Oklahoma
Oregon
Pennsylvania
Rhode Island
South Carolina
South Dakota
Tennessee
Texas
Utah
Vermont
Virginia
Washington
West Virginia
Wisconsin
Wyoming